Let's Get Healthy

Your Hair

Sarah Ridley

W
FRANKLIN WATTS
LONDON•SYDNEY

This edition first published in 2008 by Franklin Watts.

Franklin Watts
338 Euston Road
London
NW1 3BH

Franklin Watts Australia
Level 17/207 Kent Street
Sydney NSW 2000

Let's Get Healthy is a reduced text version of *Look After Yourself!*
The original texts were by Claire Llewellyn.

Series editor: Sarah Peutrill
Art director: Jonathan Hair
Design: Kirstie Billingham
Illustrations: James Evans
Photographs: Ray Moller unless otherwise acknowledged
Picture research: Diana Morris
Series consultant: Lynn Huggins-Cooper

Dewey number: 613.2
ISBN: 978 0 7496 8319 1

Printed in China

Acknowledgments:
Dr. Jeremy Burgess/Science Photo Library: 10cl
Eye of Science/Science Photo Library: 22b
Dr. Chris Hale/Science Photo Library: 24bl
Manfred Kage/Science Photo Library: 10bl
David Scharf/Science Photo Library: 8
Superstock: 21b
Andrew Syred/Science Photo Library: 24tr

With thanks to our models: Alice, Emilia, Holly, Jerome, Lewis,
Mandalena and Wilf.

Franklin Watts is a division of Hachette Children's
Books, an Hachette Livre UK company.
www.hachettelivre.co.uk

Contents

Looking at hair

There are many types of hair. Your hair may be curly or straight, thick or fine.

What's yours like?

Hair may be red, black, brown, fair, grey or white.

Your hair helps to make you look like YOU!

A head of hair

A hair is a soft thread that grows out of the skin.

This photo shows two magnified hairs growing out of the skin.

Most of us have about 100,000 hairs on our heads.

Heads get cold without hair.

About 50 hairs drop out every day. New hairs take their place.

Messy hair

My hair is a mess!

Hair often gets messy, especially overnight.

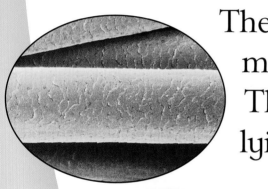

These hairs are magnified. This one is lying flat.

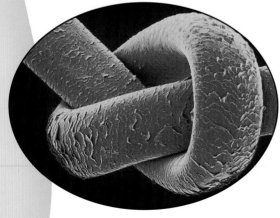

This hair is tangled.

Brushing your hair gets rid of tangles and makes the hair lie flat.

Always brush gently.

Brushes and combs

Keeping your hair tidy is easy.
All you need is a brush and comb.

Brushes and combs soon get dirty. Wash them in soapy water.

Hair gets dirty

Each hair is coated with oil. Dirt sticks to the oil, making hair dirty.

Dirty hair looks bad.

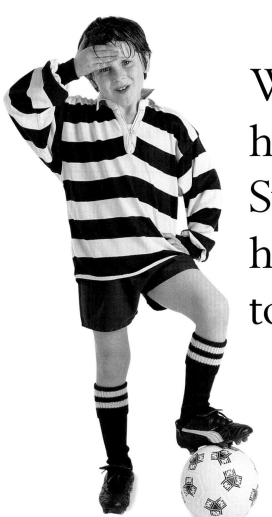

When we are hot, our heads begin to sweat. Sweat makes our hair dirty, too.

Chlorine in swimming pools harms our hair.

Wash hair after a swim.

Washing your hair

Wash hair once
or twice a week.

My hair is clean and shiny.

1 Wet the hair.

2 Pour some
shampoo
onto your
hand.

3 Rub the shampoo into your hair.

4 Rinse off the bubbles with clean water.

5 Some people use conditioner on their hair. Follow the instructions on the bottle.

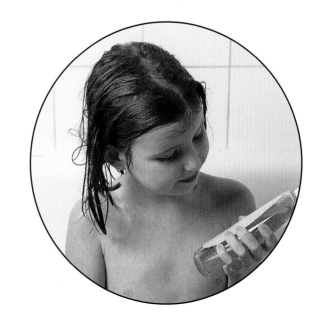

Drying your hair

Pat your wet hair with a towel. It is best to let hair dry on its own.

If you do use a hairdryer, hold it away from your head.

Ouch! Hairdryers are hot.

Thick hair takes longer to dry.

19

Hairstyles

People wear their hair in
all kinds of ways.

Look at
my hair!

Our hairstyle is one of the things that makes us look different.

What hairstyle do you have?

Having a haircut

As hair grows, the end of the hair becomes weaker.

These hairs have been magnified.

In time hairs may split.

To keep it healthy and strong, our hair needs to be cut every two months.

Hair grows more quickly in summer than winter.

This girl can see better after her haircut!

Head lice

Tiny creatures called head lice like to live in hair.

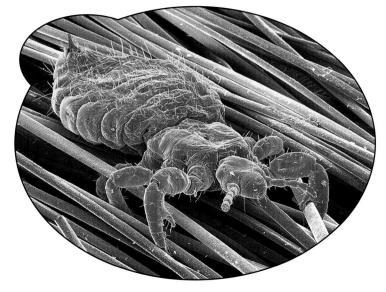

A magnified head louse

My head itches.

Their eggs (nits) look like tiny beads.

Head lice spread easily from head to head.

Most children get head lice at some time.

You need a special shampoo and comb to get rid of head lice.

Healthy hair

Everyone wants healthy hair.

Look at my shiny hair!

Eating these foods will help make your hair grow strong.

Other foods help
keep it healthy.

Drinking water
is very good for
your hair.

Remember
to wash and
brush your
hair as well.

Glossary

chlorine   A strong-smelling gas used in swimming pools to keep the water clean.

conditioner   A hair product that you put on your hair to make it soft and shiny.

fair   Having hair of a light colour.

hairstyle   The way you choose to have your hair.

head lice   (singular: **head louse**) Tiny insects that live in the hair.

magnified   Made to look bigger.

nit   The egg of a head louse.

rinse	To wash away with water.
root	The part of the hair that grows under the skin.
shampoo	A liquid soap used for washing hair.
sweat	A salty, sticky liquid produced by the skin when you are hot. It helps to cool you down.
tangle	A small knot in the hair.
thread	A very thin strand of something.

Index

About this book

Learning the principles of how to keep healthy and clean is one of life's most important skills. **Let's Get Healthy** is a series aimed at young children who are just beginning to develop these skills. **Your Hair** looks at how to keep hair clean, tidy and healthy.

Here are a number of activities children could try:

Pages 6-7 Collect photographs of people with different hair types.

Pages 8-9 Discuss how body hair helps to keep us warm — at cold temperatures hairs stand up, trapping warm air next to the skin. (As the hairs stand up we get goose pimples.)

Pages 10-11 Hold a section of hair near the root and run fingers carefully down the hair. Then do the same, but run the fingers up towards the root. With a little concentration, the hair feels smooth running down, but rough running up. This is because running fingers towards the root makes the scales stand up.

Pages 12-13 Ask children to design a comb or hairbrush that would be ideal for their own hair. Will the teeth or bristles be close or far apart, long or short? What will the handle be like?

Pages 14-15 Research the elaborate hairstyles of the 18th century. The hair was sometimes so dirty mice nested inside!

Pages 16-17 Collect a range of shampoos and conditioners and look at the instructions for using them. Are they all the same? Ask children to design their own shampoo labels. What will their shampoo do? What will it be called?

Pages 18-19 Write step-by-step instructions for using a hairdryer.

Pages 20-21 Conduct a survey of the different hairstyles in a class or group. Which is the most popular way to wear hair — short or long? What is the favourite style for long hair?

Pages 22-23 Interview a hairdresser about his or her job.

Pages 24-25 Study the lifecycle of a head louse.

Pages 26-27 Create some 'recipes for healthy hair' using the foods that are good for hair.